THE BREAK FREE WORKBOOK

STEPHANIE MCKIE

COPYRIGHT © 2023
STEPHANIE MCKIE

All rights reserved. No part of this publication may be reproduced, copied, stored in a retrieval system, transmitted, or scanned in any form or under any conditions, including, photocopying, electronic, recording, or otherwise, without the written permission of the author, Stephanie McKie.

ISBN: 978-1-954755-70-3

Published and formatted by:
Restoration of the Breach without Borders
West Palm Beach, Florida 33407
restorativeauthor@gmail.com
Tele: (561) 388-2949

Cover Design by:
Demron Anderson

TABLE OF CONTENTS

DEDICATION	1
ACKNOWLEDGMENTS	2
INTRODUCTION	3
CHAPTER 1: SPIRITUAL REALM VS NATURAL REALM	15
CHAPTER 2: THE SPIRIT OF LIMITATION	30
CHAPTER 3: STRATEGIES TO COMBAT THE SPIRIT OF SEPARATION	47
CHAPTER 4: SPIRITUAL SPOUSES	78
MISCELLANEOUS	174
MAINTENANCE	193
CONCLUSION	202
ABOUT THE AUTHOR	203
BREAKFREE PRAYER:	205
REFERENCES	206

DEDICATION

I would like to dedicate this book to all those who are fighting against some type of stronghold and need to completely break free in victory.

As you equip yourself with the knowledge and strategies laid out for you in this book, I stand with you in prayer, and I decree and declare that your life shall never be the same and that you will enter an abundance of pure greatness with acceleration.

ACKNOWLEDGMENTS

I would like to acknowledge first and foremost The Holy Spirit who is my guide, my coverage, and my comforter. Without Him, this book would not be possible. He has given me all the wisdom, knowledge, and understanding that is conveyed in this book. Holy Spirit, I thank you. I would also like to acknowledge my late father, Allan Rose Mckie. He has nurtured me with so much spiritual knowledge and prayed sincerely for me to excel in the things of God. Daddy, today you are not here to see this great accomplishment, but I can only imagine the smile that would have been on your face to see that I finally did it! I love you, Daddy, continue to take your rest. To my three children, Mommy loves you all. To Pastor Dameain Sewell, Minister Vanessa Suppria, and Dr. Chris Joseph, thank you for your continuous support. To my church family of Kingdom Power and Faith Global; Healing, Restoration, and Prophetic Ministries, thank you for your continuous prayers and encouragement to keep going on. Love you guys! KPFG STRONG!

INTRODUCTION

Let me first start by saying, we are the reflection of God, and we were created with the intent of abundant living. We are given dominion over the earth and are given the command to be fruitful, to grow and to multiply as well as to be structured and organized. The book of Genesis 1:26-28 confirms this:

And God said, "Let us make man in our image, after our likeness: and let them have dominion over the fish of the sea, and over the fowl of the air, and over the cattle, and over all the earth, and over every creeping thing that creepeth upon the earth.

So, God created man in his own image, in the image of God created he him; male and female created he them.

And God blessed them, and God said unto them, be fruitful, and multiply, and replenish the earth, and subdue it: and have dominion over the fish of the sea, and over the fowl of the air, and over every living thing that moveth upon the earth."

To grasp the profound significance of the meaning of this scripture, let us look at a couple keywords that are in this chapter. The first word is ***image***. This means, *"**a visual representation of something**"*. For example, a picture taken of someone is not the person, but it captures the image of the person. So, it shows what the person looks like without seeing him or her in real life. In this case, we are not a visual representation of God by physical appearance for God is not a human but rather Spirit. However, we are like a photograph that captures the spiritual, moral, and intellectual nature of God. So, we mirror God's divinity in our ability to actualize the unique qualities with which we have been endowed, and which make us different than all other creatures. To put in its simplest form, the sovereign God should be identifiable in us and through us. This also means that we are not just mere humans existing, but we have power and authority through our creator.

Therefore, we are a force to be reckoned with.

The second word is ***likeness*** which means, "***the fact or quality of being alike; resemblance.***" This tells us we are created to be in oneness with God. God in man and man in God. God is not a trillion miles away from us that we must go on a hunt to find him, but he is right here with us. The breath that we breathe is God's.

In fact, Isaiah 41:10 declares:

"Fear not, for I am with you;
be not dismayed, for I am your God;
I will strengthen you, I will help you,
I will uphold you with my righteous right hand."

It is God's intent to be with all men despite our backgrounds. His intention for us is to express his thoughts and represent his kingdom here on Earth. However, we must acknowledge this truth and allow His Spirit to manifest through us and his will to be done through us.

The third word to look at is **dominion.** This means, **"rule or power over."** We are to be the steward of the earth; we are to bring the material world and all its varied elements into the service of God and the good of mankind. The command to subdue the earth is a part of God's blessing on mankind. Created in the image of God, Adam and Eve were to use the earth's vast resources in the service of both God and them. It would only make sense for God to decree this since only humans were created in God's image. However, to take dominion, we must first understand who we are and the power that is given unto us. Then we must walk in obedience to the word of God. After which, we will experience true power and authority here on earth.

Now finally, let's look at the word **blessed.**

What does it mean to be blessed by God? It means, "God's favor and protection." In its simple terms, it is to be given continuous **favor** both in the spiritual and natural realms.

What is **favor**? Favor means God stepping into one's situation to make a worthwhile difference. Favor is the highway that connects you with your destiny. Favor is when it doesn't make any sense, yet it just worked out miraculously. Favor is having peace in a situation that was meant to drive you crazy. Favor is looking at a shut door in front of you and you know that you know that it's impossible to be opened but then God does it. Favor is being given a position that you are not qualified for. Genesis 1: 28, told us that man was blessed by God. This means that the way is already made clear for us despite what we see before us, God said it's already done. Therefore, understanding this, we cannot accept defeat from the adversary. Instead, we must come in agreement and alignment with the spoken word of God and take authority over what has been given unto us. **Luke 10:19 tells us,**

"Behold, I give unto you power to tread on serpents and scorpions, and over all the power of the enemy: and nothing shall by any means hurt you."

We must believe this scripture and start to use the power and authority that he has given us to defeat the enemy's plans for our lives. What is that power and authority? His word!

We Are spiritual beings in mortal bodies

Who are we?

Each one of us is unique; we come from various backgrounds and have different personalities but with respect to how God created us, we are actually all the same. We are spirits given a soul and a body.

The Bible tells us in **1 Thessalonians 5:23:**

"And the very God of peace sanctify you wholly; and I pray God your whole spirit and soul and body be preserved blameless unto the coming of our Lord Jesus Christ".

This passage strongly indicates that man is of three parts: **spirit**, **soul**, and **body**. The **spirit** as our inmost part is the inner organ, possessing God-consciousness, that we may contact God (John 4:24: God is a Spirit: and they that worship him must worship him in spirit and in truth, Romans 1:19: because that which is known about God is evident within them; for God made it evident to them).

The Bible mentions the human spirit numerous times.

From the very beginning, the Bible reveals God made human beings with three parts, including a spirit. Genesis 2:7 says:

"Then God formed man from the dust of the ground and breathed into his nostrils the breath of life, and man became a living soul."

God formed man's physical **body** with the dust of the ground. Then God breathed into his nostrils, and man became a living **soul**.

Now, where is the human spirit in this verse? We don't see the words human spirit, but what we do see is the breath of life. In Hebrew, the original language of the Old Testament, the word translated as *breath* is *neshamah*. This same Hebrew word is translated as *spirit* in Proverbs 20:27, which says:

"The spirit of man is the lamp of Jehovah."

By this we can see that when God breathed into man, man's **human spirit** came into existence. Our human spirit is the deepest part of our being.

But why did God create us with a human spirit? Isn't having a body and soul enough for us to exist?

Why we have a spirit

Our spirit was created by God so that we can **contact** and **receive** Him.

Our body and our soul have their own specific functions, only our spirit has the ability to contact God. We can see this in numerous verses, including John 4:24:

"God is Spirit, and those who worship Him must worship in spirit and truthfulness."

To contact—or worship—God, who is Spirit, we must use our spirit. The way a radio function is a good illustration of our spirit's unique ability to contact and receive God. When a radio is turned on and properly tuned, it can receive invisible radio waves in the air and interpret them.

Our human spirit is like a radio, and God is like the radio waves. Our spirit is the part of our being that corresponds to what God is, so we must use our spirit to contact Him.

Now let's look at the explanation of our soul:

"The **soul** is our very self (*Matt. 16:26; For what good will it do a person if he gains the whole world, but forfeits his soul? Or what will a person give in exchange for his soul? Luke 9:25; For what good does it do a person if he gains the whole world, but loses or forfeits himself*), a medium between our spirit and our body, possessing self-consciousness, that we may have our personality."

Our soul perceives things in the psychological realm. In fact, in Greek—the original language of the New Testament—the word for *soul* is *psuche*, which is also the root word of *psychology*.

Our soul is our personality, who we are. With our soul, we think, reason, consider, remember, and wonder. We experience emotions like happiness, love, sorrow, anger, relief, and compassion. And we're able to resolve, choose, and make decisions.

Now let's look at our body and how our three parts are related:

"The **body** as our external part is the outer organ, possessing world-consciousness, that we may contact the material world. The body contains the soul, and the soul is the vessel that contains the spirit."

Our body exists in and contacts the tangible things of the material world using our five physical senses. The body is the visible, external part of our being, and it contains the soul. Our soul is the vessel containing our spirit.

Below is a simple diagram of three concentric circles illustrating these three parts. It shows the body as our outer, visible part, the soul as our inward part, and our spirit as our innermost, hidden part.

So, we understand that we are spiritual beings that are connected to both the spiritual and natural realms. We have the capability to access information in the spiritual realms by the Spirit of God, the Holy Spirit, before things manifest and/or while they are manifesting in the natural. The book Ezekiel chapter 1 declares:

"Now it came to pass in the thirtieth year, in the fourth month, in the fifth day of the month, as I was among the captives by the river of Chebar, that the heavens were opened, and I saw visions of God".

What does he mean by the heavens were open? This means that he got access to see in the realms of the spirit. As access was granted to him, he began to see visions of God. Seeing visions of God means having revelations of the spiritual, divine, and heavenly things, and this requires an open heaven.

To have divine visions and have them consistently, we must be like Ezekiel, be open to the Lord, seek, contacting the Lord, and be one with the Lord.

Why is spiritual information important?

It is important for the will of God to be carried out on earth.

Understanding the Unity of Spiritual and Earthy Realms

Everything Starts in The Spiritual Realm Before We See It in The Physical Realm. First, we must know that the earth is governed by the spirit world. What we see manifesting on earth whether good or bad, is a product of what is in the spirit. Therefore, everything first happens in the spirit realm before manifesting to the earth realm.

John 4:24 Says, **"God is Spirit, and those who worship him must worship in spirit and truth"** And in Genesis

1:1 Says, ***"In the beginning God created the heavens and the earth."***

From this, we gain the knowledge that the earth is natural/physical, but God is Spirit; we understand that someone spiritual created something natural. The physical world came from the spirit world. Also, the greater reality is spiritual; when we look at physical things, we should be reminded how powerful the spiritual realm is. Everything physical has its origin in the spirit; physical things are dependent upon spiritual things for their existence!

Ephesians 1:3 Says, ***"Blessed be the God and father of our Lord Jesus Christ, who has blessed us with every spiritual blessing in the heavenly places in Christ."***

Because everything has its origin in the spirit, We must deal with every situation in the spirit before dealing with it in the physical. That is why God has blessed us with everything, first in the heavenly realm. We can claim and exercise our spiritual authority only to the extent that we are operating in the realm of the spirit.

CHAPTER 1
SPIRITUAL REALM VS NATURAL REALM

In Hebrews 12:18-24, we see the contrast between these two environments. Mount Zion represents the heavenly realm.

Hebrews 12:18-24:

"For you have not come to a mountain that can be touched and to a blazing fire, and to darkness and gloom and whirlwind, and to the blast of a trumpet and the sound of words, which sound was such that those who heard begged that no further word be spoken to them. For they could not cope with the command, "If even an animal touches the mountain, it shall be stoned." And so terrible was the sight, that Moses said, "I am terrified and trembling." But you have come to Mount Zion and to the city of the living God, the heavenly Jerusalem, and to myriads of angels, to the general assembly and church of the firstborn who are enrolled in heaven, and to God, the Judge of all, and to the spirits of the righteous made perfect, and to Jesus, the mediator of a new covenant, and to the sprinkled blood, which speaks better than the blood of Abel".

STEPHANIE MCKIE

SPIRITUAL WARFARE

Research and answer the following question:

Please support your answers with scriptures.

What is spiritual warfare?

Now that we understand what spiritual warfare is and we are fully aware that everything is spiritual and that what we see on earth is a product of the spirit realm, we now understand that the battles that we experience are also spiritual despite how they may seem otherwise. Ephesians 6:12 says,

"For we wrestle not against flesh and blood, but against principalities, against powers, against the rulers of the darkness of this world, against spiritual wickedness in high places".

To Do:

Research and answer the following questions:

Please support your answers with scriptures.

What are principalities?

....
....
....
....
....
....
....
....

What are the powers Paul is talking about?

Who are the rulers of the darkness of this world?

....
....
....
....
....

What is spiritual wickedness in high places?

....
....
....
....
....
....
....
....
....
....

This scripture is a master key that is given unto us to unlock spiritual power that will give us victory in warfare. Once we understand that the fight is not between us but rather against the devil and other evil forces, our approach will be governed by the spiritual knowledge that is given to us to be successful in this fight.

Just like how God is a Spirit, and we are also spirits, the devil is a spirit as well and the bible tells us that the devil is our adversary (***1 Peter 5:8 "Be of sober spirit, be on the alert. Your adversary, the devil, prowls around like a roaring lion, seeking someone to devour"***).

Therefore, if our enemy is also spiritual, it simply means that the war that he rages against us is spiritual as well. So even though we experience the battles in the natural, it is a result of the schemes he raises against us in the realm of the spirit. Again, it all happens in the spiritual realm. No matter the circumstance, no matter how it may come across in the natural, it is a replica of the spirit realm. Therefore, understand that to fight against the schemes of the devil and be victorious, it must be fought in the spirit.

The book of Revelation 12:7-17 confirms this:

Now war arose in heaven, Michael and his angels fighting against the dragon; and the dragon and his angels fought, but they were defeated and there was no longer any place for them in heaven. And the great dragon was thrown down, that ancient

serpent, who is called the Devil and Satan, the deceiver of the whole world—he was thrown down to the earth, and his angels were thrown down with him. And I heard a loud voice in heaven, saying, "Now the salvation and the power and the kingdom of our God and the authority of his Christ have come, for the accuser of our brethren has been thrown down, who accuses them day and night before our God. And they have conquered him by the blood of the Lamb and by the word of their testimony, for they loved not their lives even unto death. Rejoice then, O heaven and you that dwell therein! But woe to you, O earth and sea, for the devil has come down to you in great wrath, because he knows that his time is short!" And when the dragon saw that he had been thrown down to the earth, he pursued the woman who had borne the male child. But the woman was given the two wings of the great eagle that she might fly from the serpent into the wilderness, to the place where she is to be nourished for a time, and times, and half a time. The serpent poured water like a river out of his mouth after the woman, to sweep her away with the flood. But the earth came to the help of the woman, and the earth opened its mouth and swallowed the river which the dragon had poured from his mouth. Then the dragon was angry with the woman and went off to make war on the rest of her offspring, on those who keep the commandments of God and bear testimony to Jesus. And he stood on the sand of the sea.

Here we see that a war took place in the spiritual realm/heaven against the angels of God and the dragon who is the devil, which the angels of God won. But What was the reason for this war?

Let's look at Mathew Chapter 2:

"Now when Jesus was born in Bethlehem of Judaea in the days of Herod the king, behold, there came wise men from the east to Jerusalem, Saying, where is he that is born King of the Jews? for we have seen his star in the east, and are come to worship him.

When Herod the king had heard these things, he was troubled, and all Jerusalem with him. And when he had gathered all the chief priests and scribes of the people together, he demanded of them where Christ should be born. And they said unto him, In Bethlehem of Judaea: for thus it is written by the prophet, and thou Bethlehem, in the land of Juda, art not the least among the princes of Juda: for out of thee shall come a Governor, that shall rule my people Israel.

Then Herod, when he had privily called the wise men, enquired of them diligently what time the star appeared. And he sent them to Bethlehem, and said, Go and search diligently for the young child; and when ye have found him, bring me word again, that I may come and worship him also. When they had heard the king, they departed; and, lo, the star, which they saw in the east, went before them, till it came and stood over where the young child was. When they saw the star, they rejoiced with exceeding great joy. And when they were come into the house, they saw the young child with Mary his mother, and fell down, and worshipped him: and when they had opened their treasures, they presented unto him gifts; gold, and frankincense and myrrh.

And being warned of God in a dream that they should not return to Herod, they departed into their own country another way.

And when they were departed, behold, the angel of the Lord appeareth to Joseph in a dream, saying, Arise, and take the young child and his mother, and flee into Egypt, and be thou there until I bring thee word: for Herod will seek the young child to destroy him.

When he arose, he took the young child and his mother by night and departed into Egypt: And was there until the death of Herod: that it might be fulfilled which was spoken of the Lord by the *prophet, saying, Out of Egypt have I called my son. Then Herod, when he saw that he was mocked of the wise men, was exceeding wroth, and sent forth, and slew all the children that were in Bethlehem, and in all the coasts thereof, from two years old and under, according to the time which he had diligently inquired of the wise men. Then was fulfilled that which was spoken by Jeremiah the prophet, saying, In Rama was there a voice heard, lamentation, and weeping, and great mourning, Rachel weeping for her children, and would not be comforted, because they are not. But when Herod was dead, behold, an angel of the Lord appeareth in a dream to Joseph in Egypt, Saying, Arise, and take the young child and his mother, and go into the land of Israel: for they are dead which sought the young child's life. And he arose, and took the young child and his mother, and came into the land of Israel. But when he heard that Archelaus did reign in Judaea in the room of his father Herod, he was afraid to go thither: notwithstanding, being warned of God in a dream, he turned aside into the parts of Galilee: And he came and dwelt in a city called Nazareth: that it might be fulfilled which was spoken by the prophets, He shall be called a Nazarene."*

When we examine both scriptures, we see a spiritual war that was fought in heaven (Revelation 12: 7-10) and the angels of God defeated the devil. After his defeat, he attacked the child born of a woman. Years later in Mathew chapter two, we see the earthly manifestation of the attack. These two chapters also confirm that the spiritual governs the natural.

As we read these two scriptures, understand that this is exactly how the fight is done in the spiritual realm against our lives, sometimes even years ago before it manifests itself.

If we focus on the natural and try to fight a spirit in the natural, we shall certainly fail. Many people have been doing this for years, fighting spiritual battles in the natural world, hence, the reason they are still fighting today. However, they are taking the wrong approach and need to redirect their focus to the real source, the enemy.

The reason why the war appears to be against our fellow humans is because, just like how we are connected to the Spirit of God, and he uses us to carry out his will on earth, some people through disobedience to the way of God, have made themselves readily available for the devil to use them. Therefore, their behavior now becomes a product of the spirit of the devil.

So, in essence, you are fighting against the spirit that has overtaken them and not the individual him or herself. However, that person can turn from being disobedient to God's will and repent. He or she can be delivered from being guided or controlled by that evil spirit and will no longer operate by its schemes. That's why an ex-murderer who accepts Jesus Christ can become a powerful man or woman of God because he or she has been released from the spirit of murder and is now operating by the Spirit of God.

What are the or Schemes/Wiles of the Devil?

Ephesians 6-11 says:

"Put on the full armor of God, so that you will be able to stand firm against the schemes of the devil."

The King James version reads:

"Put on the whole armour of God, that ye may be able to stand against the wiles of the devil."

Let's look at a few definitions:

Scheme:

To make plans, especially in a devious way or with intent to do something illegal or wrong.

Wiles:

devious or cunning **stratagems** *employed in manipulating or persuading someone to do what one wants.*

Stratagems:

a plan or scheme, especially one used to outwit an opponent or achieve an end.

From the definitions of these words, what is your understanding of the operation of the enemy against us?

....
....
....
....
....
....
....
....
....
....
....
....
....
....

....
....
....
....
....
....
....
....
....
....
....
....
....
....
....
....

Let's look at some stratagems, schemes, or wiles that the devil and these evil forces try to use to destroy or block our divine destinies.

CHAPTER 2

THE SPIRIT OF LIMITATION

We are going to look at the definition of the spirit of limitation then we are going to break it down into several components.

The word limitation means:

A limiting condition; restrictive weakness; lack of capacity; inability or handicap.

The spirit of limitation is popularly used by the devil and his agents to block or limit one's advancement into his or her divine destiny. The spirit of limitation is also used to displace an individual from his or her true position, responsibilities, and purpose, causing instability and uncertainty of one's identity.

The spirit of limitation has many components or other spirits attached to it. Let's look at some of these other spirits. The spirit of separation, isolation, or exile.

What is the function of this spirit and why it is a necessary weapon of the enemy?

There is a saying, "together we stand, but divided we fall". This saying has been proven to be very true.

There is strength and power in unity. However, when there is a separation among a people whether it's in the family, church, business, etc., it can come with serious implications such as instability, bitterness, displacements, disfunction, incapability, mental disorders and the list goes on. Of course, we know that some separations are necessary and must be made, but some are schemes by the enemies to cause hindrance to the parties involved.

Let's look at a scenario of the adverse effect of separation among a family.

Let's imagine a married couple with two children living together in a home that is quite functional and has a proper structure in place that guides the family along a positive and productive path. What we can assume here is that we will see strong healthy morals and core values that will have a great impact on the lives of many and society at large. Now, let's imagine the spirit of separation steps in. What we will possibly now see is that a family that was once so beautiful becomes displaced, dysfunctional and can no longer feed or promote a healthy lifestyle among itself nor even to others. Therefore, the purpose of that family will now become restricted or limited. We are not going to say the purpose is aborted because there is always the opportunity for restoration through Jesus Christ.

Mark Chapter 3: 25 declares.

"If a house is divided against itself, that house cannot stand."

With this verse, we see the reason why the spirit of separation is a powerful tool for the enemies to use against us because separation can cause a downfall.

When the enemy wants to launch an attack or destroy the purpose in someone's life, he first tries to separate that individual from his or her support system so that the individual becomes weak and if not quickly offered the proper aid, will become susceptible to the devil's wiles.

The spirit of separation is very dangerous. It limits you and can even have a deadly impact on you whether spiritually or physically. When the devil causes one to be separated, isolated or exiled, then he can throw brutal punches at you, that can have damning effect. For example, his demons will pollute you with thoughts of you being a failure, disappointment, good for nothing, etc. This is then followed depression. Which may result in spiritual depletion. Once this happens, the demons of suicide, anger, hatred, bitterness, murder, etc., comes in to eliminate you; and many times, without the intervention of others and God's divine power, the enemies will win.

SIGNS THAT YOU MIGHT BE BATTLING WITH THE SPIRIT OF SEPARATION.

- Consistent lack of interest to be around others who would normally encourage or help you to grow in your purpose
- Extended periods of withdrawn from family, friends, etc.

- Thoughts that you don't need anyone's help for you to succeed
- Loss of interest to communicate with others
- The sudden feeling of wanting to be by yourself
- Inexplainable feelings of sadness, bitterness, etc.
- Thoughts or believe that everyone is against you
- Thoughts that your life or existence doesn't matter
- Any other feeling that will cause you to isolate yourself from others

Today, I encourage you, do not be a victim to the spirit of separation. If you are reading this book and you can identify with some of the symptoms or symptom above, I want you to first write down what you are experiencing at this time in the space provided below. Why writing this down is important? It gives you a clearer picture of what's going on in your life. It also helps you to analyze the situation from a different perspective and helps you to make an appropriate decision to find the proper solution to what you are experiencing. It also helps you to remember what to specifically pray about when you are praying. This is the first step towards your Break Free – **Acknowledgement.**

Do you Acknowledge that you are experiencing symptoms of the spirit of separation?

Circle One

Yes, or No?

If yes, what are the symptoms?

....
....
....
....
....
....
....
....
....

ACCEPTANCE

Once you acknowledge that you are battling with the spirit of separation, the next step is accepting it. Sometimes acceptance is difficult, especially for those persons who seek for guidance, or if you are in a certain revered position or if you are being held to a high standard. This can make you feel guilty and obligated to think that you are okay so you can appear okay to the people who are depending on you; so, you don't want to accept that you are in a battle and that you need help. When this happens, it limits the possibilities for change or solution. Therefore, as bad as the situation may be, acceptance plays a great role for your Beak Free.

Please write out your acceptance declaration in the space provided below.

....
....
....
....
....
....
....
....
....
....
....
....
....
....
....
....
....
....
....
....

ANALYZE THE MAGNITUDE OF YOUR SITUATION

After you have accepted your situation, you will need to analyze the severity of it. This will help you understand where you are and the level of help that is needed to Break Free.

Understand this, there are levels of demonic ranks. Some are higher in rank than others. Hence, their powers and authority flow differently. For example, if you are experiencing the spirit of limitation but you find that you have prayed a couple times and you are overcoming or were able to overcome its assignment, it might be that you are or were dealing with a demon whose power is no match to the level of anointing that you carry. However, you can have a high-ranking demon that is very strong in power that you are not able to manage to fight on your own. Therefore, you will need help from someone to match that demon. So, it is important to know the level where you are spiritually and what is the magnitude of the situation so you can get the proper help needed to Break Free.

Please write out Daniel Chapter 10:12-13:

....
....
....
....
....
....
....
....
....
....
....
....
....
....

What is your understanding of this scripture?

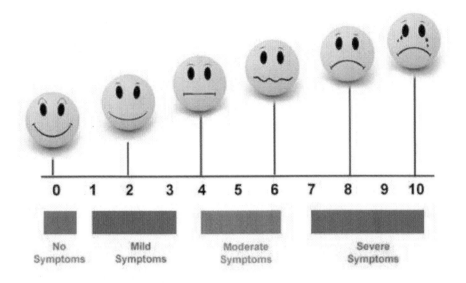

TIME TO ANALYZE ON A SCALE OF ZERO TO TEN, WITH ONE BEING THE LEAST AND TEN BEING THE MAX, HOW DO YOU EVALUATE YOUR SITUATION?

Please circle one below

Answer:

- A) No Symptoms
- B) Mild Symptoms
- C) Moderate Symptoms
- D) Severe Symptoms

Now that you know what level you are at, it's time to put strategies in place to deal with the issue appropriately.

Please understand that breaking free is not just going to happen by itself. You must be determined to put in the work. It won't be easy, but you must be intentional and relentless to Break Free.

Demons are relentless and so should we. Let's look at Luke chapter 8:26-29.

Research the scripture Luke Chapter 8: 26-29:

Write it out in the space provided below:

....
....
....
....
....
....
....
....
....
....
....
....
....
....
....
....

....
....
....

In verses 27 notice it said the demon caused the young man to live not in a house but in tombs for a long time. Secondly, did you also notice in verse 29 it states that the boy was driven to the wilderness by demons?

What do you know about the wilderness?

....
....
....
....
....
....
....
....
....
....
....
....
....
....

Please understand that this spirit drives people into spiritual and even physical wilderness by controlling one's mindset. Therefore, it is imperative that one's mind is consistently being renewed by the word of God.

Romans 12:2 declares:

"And be not conformed to this world: but be ye transformed by the renewing of your mind, that ye may prove what is that good, and acceptable, and perfect, will of God."

Now, let's explores some ways to Break Free from the spirit of separation/isolation.

BREAK FREE FROM THE SPIRIT OF SEPARATION/ISOLATION

CHAPTER 3
STRATEGIES TO COMBAT THE SPIRIT OF SEPARATION

Understand that in the spirit realm there are orders and strategies in place. Therefore, if we are going to be successful in combating the wiles of the enemies, it also means that we must plan to be successful in this conquest.

- ***Firstly***, always remember that life is spiritual and needs spiritual intervention to deal with its manifestations in the natural world. With that being said, we will start with **PRAYER**. Why Prayer? Because prayer goes where our feet cannot go. However, there are certain types of prayer that are required for certain battles. This is where the mystery unfolds. Many people have been praying for years to break strong holds and seem to be getting nowhere and that can be a result of lack of understanding of the spirit they are dealing with and lack understanding of how to pray strategically to break those strong holds. In this case we understand the functions of the spirit we are dealing with. So, with that, we are going to address it by its name and the symptoms currently being experienced.
- ***Secondly***, we are going to use scripture to speak against this spirit. Psalms 91 vs 4 declares*: **"He shall cover thee with his feathers, and under his wings shalt thou trust: his truth shall be thy shield and buckler"**. His Truth is His word.
- ***Thirdly***, the recommended times to pray regarding these matters are **12:00am-3:00am**. This time frame is the Breaking of Day

This is a period of spiritual activity. This watch hour will strengthen your faith. It is the same time that Peter denied Christ three times.

This watch is also known as the witching hour. This watch is the darkest and most demonic part of the night, especially at midnight. Witches, warlocks, and Satanists have fun and start their incantations during this part of the night. The devil operates at this time because this is the time that men are in a deep sleep and there are not as many people praying to oppose him (1 Kings 3:20). Therefore, this is the best time to pray to intercept and reverse demonic actives. This watch also calls for seasoned intercessors to pray consistently.

Research and Write out Acts 16: 24-25

....
....
....
....
....
....
....
....
....

STEPHANIE MCKIE

- **Fourthly**, we are going on some intentional fasting- We should seek the leading of the Holy Spirit on the number of days for fasting to deal with this specific matter.

The first day of fasting should always be about repentance, consecration, and sanctification of oneself. This paves the way for God to hear us and to answer and move on our behalf.

We can pray individually and corporately. However, everyone who is assigned on this mission must be of one accord and follow the instructions of the Holy Spirit accurately.

THE IMPORTANCE OF FASTING

- Often in the Bible, God's people fasted immediately before a major victory, miracle, or answer to prayer. It prepared them for a blessing!
- Moses fasted before he received the Ten Commandments. "Moses was there with the Lord forty days and forty nights without eating bread or drinking water. And he wrote on the tablets the words of the covenant--the "Ten Commandments." Exodus 34:28 (NIV)
- The Israelites fasted before a miraculous victory. "Some men came and told Jehoshaphat, "A vast army is coming against you from Edom, from the other side of the Sea. It is already in Hazazon Tamar" (that is, En Gedi). Alarmed, Jehoshaphat resolved to inquire of the Lord, and he proclaimed a fast for all Judah." 2 Chronicles 20:2-3 (NIV) 2
- Daniel fasted in order to receive guidance from God. "So, I turned to the Lord God and pleaded with him in prayer and petition, in fasting, and in sackcloth and ashes." Daniel 9:3 (NIV) "While I was still in prayer, Gabriel, the man I had seen in the earlier vision, came to me in swift flight about the time of the evening sacrifice. He instructed me and said to me, 'Daniel, I have now come to give you insight and understanding.'" Daniel 9:21-22 (NIV)

- Nehemiah fasted before beginning a major building project. "When I heard these things, I sat down and wept. For some days I mourned and fasted and prayed before the God of heaven." Nehemiah 1:4 (NIV)
- Jesus fasted during His victory over temptation. "For forty wilderness days and nights he was tested by the Devil. He ate nothing during those days, and when the time was up, he was hungry." Luke 4:2 (Msg)
- The first Christians fasted during-decision making times. "While they were worshiping the Lord and fasting, the Holy Spirit said, 'Set apart for me Barnabas and Saul for the work to which I have called them.' So, after they had fasted and prayed, they placed their hands on them and sent them off." Acts 13:2-3 (NIV)

While you are fasting, ensure that you are glorifying God in the process. Don't just fast because you have an issue that you want God to resolve, but fast with the intention to be one with God. In this way, God will honor your petition unto him.

Psalms 91: 1 declares, **"He *that dwelleth in the secret place of the most High shall abide under the shadow of the Almighty.*"**

The secret place of the most high is a place where you can experience the presence of God in a unique way while in prayer and fasting; when we are in his presence, no harm come near us. This is also confirmed in the same chapter verses 9-10

9" Because thou hast made the Lord, which is my refuge, even the most High, thy habitation;

10 "There shall no evil befall thee, neither shall any plague come nigh thy dwelling."

Habitation and dwelling are referring to the presence of God.

How to eat while fasting:

There are many types of fasts, and the option you choose depends upon your health, the desired length of your fast, and your preference:

- A Water Fast - means to abstain from all food and juices
- A Partial Fast - means to eliminate certain foods or specific meals
- A Vegetable Fast - means eating strictly vegetables
- A "Juice" Fast - means to drink only fruit or vegetable juices during mealtimes. I know the prospect of going without food for an extended period of time may be of concern to some, but there

are ways to ensure that your body is getting the nutrients it needs, so you can remain safe and healthy during your fast.

Next, having FAITH and being OBEDIENT.

This is a crucial step to Break Free. Prayer is communication and communication involves speaking and listening. Therefore, we must listen to what the Holy Spirit has to say. Once we hear the instructions of the Holy Spirit, we must believe and by our beliefs we act, which is Faith. Faith is hearing the word of God, believing the Word of God, and acting according to the word/instructions of God.

Please know that often times the instructions from God won't be what we want to do, but it is what we need to do to Break Free.

Look at 2 Kings 5: 1-14

What does it say?

………………………………………………………………………………
………………………………………………………………………………
………………………………………………………………………………
………………………………………………………………………………
………………………………………………………………………………

EXECUTION

Time to execute your strategies to break free

....
....
....
....
....
....
....
....
....
....

Okay, time to put what we have learned into action.

Follow the Break Free Prayer guide below.

BREAK FREE PRAYER GUIDE:

- Acknowledge Him as your father who is in heaven, Mathew 6-9: **"After this manner therefore pray ye: Our Father which art in heaven,**
- Give him praise and worship, **hallowed be thy name".**
- Thank Him, Psalms 95: 2 **"Let us come before his presence with thanksgiving",**

These steps take you in the presence of God.

- Confess your sins, and sincerely repent before Him Proverbs 28:13 **"He that covereth his sins shall not prosper: but whoso confesseth and forsaketh them shall have mercy".**
- Always pray in the name of Jesus Christ of Nazareth. John 14 **"And whatsoever ye shall ask in my name, that will I do, that the Father may be glorified in the Son".**
- Father in the name of Jesus Christ of Nazareth, I acknowledge and accept that I am battling with the spirit of separation (or any other spirits), and it is causing (list symptoms). Lord, according to your

Word in Luke chapter 10:19 ***you have given unto me power to tread on serpents and scorpions, and over all the power of the enemy: and nothing shall by any means hurt me.***

- Therefore, with this power that you have given unto me (which is His Word/the sword of the living God) I decree and declare Isaiah chapter 54:17 against the spirit of separation/isolation (or any other spirits battling with) that none of its weapon formed against me, my mind shall prosper, and its tongue which rises against me in judgment it shall be condemn. This is my heritage because I am a servant of the Lord, and my righteousness is from HIM," says the Lord. (This is why confession and repentance are very important so the Word can be true in our lives and work for us. NB: the word/power of God can only work for us when we are in right standing with God.)

- Denouncing the spirit/spirits you are battling with: Father, I come in agreement with 1 John 4:4***: that I am his dear child, is from God and have overcome them, because the one who is in me is greater than the one who is in the world"***. Therefore, with the power of Jesus Christ and by your word Lord, I denounce from my life (name the spirit/spirits), I break every covenant that I formed with you knowingly and unknowingly to me, in the mighty name of Jesus Christ of Nazareth.

- Father according to Mark *16:17* you declared ***that these signs shall follow them that believe; In your name shall I cast out devils; and shall speak with new tongues.***

- Father in the name of Jesus Christ of Nazareth, I believe in your power, I believe in your son Jesus Christ of Nazareth therefore, I CAST OUT this spirit of separation/isolation (list any other spirits you may be battling and their symptoms) from my life.

- Shut the door and decline access to this spirit or spirits: Job 38: 8-11 declares: "***Or who shut up the sea with doors, when it brake forth as if it had issued out of the womb? When I made the cloud the garment thereof, and thick darkness a swaddling band for it, 10 And brake up for it my decreed place, and set bars and doors, 11 And said, Hitherto shalt thou come, but no further: and here shall thy proud waves be stayed***"? Father, we come in agreement with your word, and we shut every open door on this spirit (name the spirit) that it may not enter in my life again.

- Any other words the Holy Spirit directs you to pray.

- Offer up thanksgiving for victory against this spirit, worship and praise Him.

Side note:

The enemies will cause a fight or disagreement between you and others so that the spirit of separation can come in. In this case, you might feel the need to separate yourself from them which is necessary. However, how do you know if this is in fact the enemy at work or not?

You be sure, you would want to do some homework before making the decision to isolate yourself from them.

- First thing first – PRAY: Always pray and seek the Lord's direction before making any move. However, before asking God's direction, you must first confess to Him what transpired, repent from any anger, unforgiveness, etc.

Please write out Mark Chapter 11: 25-26:

....
....
....

- Once that is done, continue with your prayer in seeking God on what to do and The Holy Spirit will lead you in all truth and will save you from the brutish plans of the enemy.
- Seek wise and Godly counsel: This is very important and will save you a lot of problems.
- Ask the party or parties involved to have a discussion of what transpired. Discuss peaceably and respectfully. You will be surprised to know how powerful talking about the situation is to bring healing and reconciliation.

Please write out Mathew Chapter 5:23-24:

....
....
....
....
....
....
....
....
....
....
....
....

OTHER SPIRITS OF LIMITATIONS

SPIRIT OF REJECTION

The spirit of rejection is an oppressive spirit. It robs you of joy and peace.

Oppression is defined as *mental pressure or distress*. Therefore, if the spirit of rejection is an oppressive spirit; you can think of it as a tactic by the enemy to push or press you down into the moods or emotions that block you from experiencing freedom and the presence of God's love in your life.

Does this mean that God's love has left you? The Bible says that God's love will never fail (see Psalm 136). Therefore, you must be able to discern what you feel from what is true. This comes from understanding the strategies the enemy uses in the spiritual realm.

When you understand that the spirit of rejection lies about God's love and your worth, you can begin the process of being set free. The enemy uses the stronghold of rejection in spiritual warfare, but the Word of God can work in your life to set you free.

Let's discover...

- How the spirit of rejection is manifested in your life
- Where the spirit of rejection comes from
- How to battle the spirit of rejection with the guidance of the Holy Spirit

The spirit of rejection taunts you with feelings of worthlessness. This stronghold of rejection makes you question your identity in Christ Jesus and tells you that you are not fully adopted into God's family. It battles against the spirit of sonship. It always makes you feel like you don't belong or wanted in your family or relationships.

Symptoms of the spirt of rejection:

- You feel despondent. There seems to be no words of encouragement that can be spoken over you to set you free from this feeling of rejection.
- You feel left out of conversations as if you are an observer, unable to interact.
- You feel that life's opportunities have passed you by, and it is too late to do anything about it.
- You feel rejected if you are not recognized for your accomplishments by those in authority.
- You feel the spirit of envy setting in as you begin comparing your situations with others.

- The feeling of envy and comparison partner with rejection and tell you that you were not given a fair chance in life.
- You feel the need to prove yourself while at the same time feeling you can never measure up.

Do any of these feelings resonate with you? Understand this: There is spiritual warfare happening in your mind, will, and emotions. Though this spiritual stronghold is cleaver, it does not compare to the power and love of Christ Jesus. It is His blood that was shed for you, and it will overcome the spirit of rejection.

Write out 1 John 4:3-4 in the space below:

....
....
....
....
....
....
....
....
....
....
....

To understand how the spirit of rejection operates, you must first realize that a battle is going on. You have already taken this critical first step!

It is caused by all or any one of the following:

- Neglect
- Selfishness
- Physical, emotional, and sexual abuse
- Drug use
- Repeated negative words and messages
- Broken marriages and families
- Inability to accept parental roles

Understand that this all takes place in the spiritual realm. Ephesians 6 says that we are not in war with flesh and blood, but with the principalities, powers, and rulers of the darkness in heavenly places (see Ephesians 6:12).

John 10:10 tells us that these oppressive spirits from the enemy come to steal, kill, and destroy. They do this by persecuting you through your thoughts and bringing on fears and negative mindsets full of anxiety and depression.

Do you Acknowledge that you are experiencing symptoms of the spirit of Rejection?

Circle One

Yes, or No?

If yes, what are the symptoms?

....
....
....
....
....
....
....
....
....

Please write out your acceptance declaration in the space provided below.

....
....
....
....
....
....
....
....
....
....

THE BREAK FREE WORKBOOK

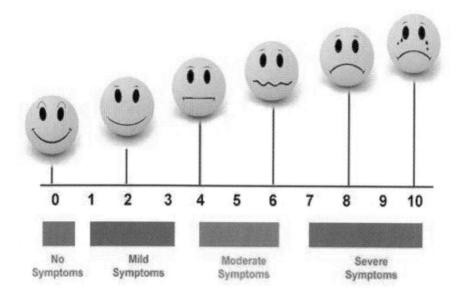

ZERO BEING THE LEAST AND TEN BEING THE MAX, HOW DO YOU EVALUATE YOUR SITUATION?

Please circle one below:

Answer:

- A) No Symptoms
- B) Mild Symptoms
- C) Moderate Symptoms
- D) Severe Symptoms

EXECUTION

Time to execute your strategies to break free

....
....
....
....
....
....
....
....
....
....
....

TO BREAK FREE FROM THE SPIRIT OF REJECTION

Follow the Break Free Prayer guide

Additional Steps

- Prayerfully ask the Holy Spirit to reveal the root cause of this oppressive spirit.
- Declare your identity in Christ.
- Stay in the Word of God. Remember, in consistency lies victory! Spend time with God daily and meditate, filling your mind with who He says you are.
- Thank God for all He has done and will do as He promises to set you free!

CHAPTER 4

SPIRITUAL SPOUSES

Ask anyone who has been in the deliverance ministry about spiritual spouses and almost every person will tell you that they have encountered a "spirit spouse" case.

Many people can tell you of an encounter they've had with these spirits.

Spiritual spouses like Incubus, Succubus, or Lilith not only attack a person with sexual encounters and physical molestation but also impregnate him/her with spiritual perversion or confusion.

Isaiah 34:14 says, **"The wild beasts of the desert shall also meet with the jackals, and the wild goat shall bleat to its companion; Also, the night creature shall rest there, and find for herself a place of rest."**

While some Bible translations mention "Lilith" directly, the others provide a footnote in reference to the night creature as Lilith, a night demon who is a sexual wanton.

We also see in Genesis 6, that spiritual entities came to earth and had physical relationships with human women and had offspring – the Nephilim.

Research: Who Were the Nephilim?

Write the findings below:

....
....
....
....
....
....
....
....
....
....
....
....
....
....
....
....
....
....
....

These demons continue to have sex with humans, and although their offspring are not actual babies, this act still produces physical effects in people's lives. Some dreams are more violent in nature than others, so much so that people wake up with either an orgasm, feeling physically violated, raped, tortured, tormented, and even emotionally drained from these encounters. The "offspring" of these encounters almost always last throughout the day, and oftentimes they destroy relationships, marriages, a person's peace, and even their ability to function. These wet dreams, spiritual orgasms, and torments at times become addictive and are usually followed by guilt, condemnation, and accusation.

These demons delight in inflicting pain, fear, and mental anguish. Ultimately, they seek to destroy the abundant life created by God.

Through repeated sexual encounters, they attach themselves to the people and hinder their relationship with another human. As a result, the person experiences these signs:

- Battle with consistent wet dreams or dreams induced orgasms.
- Feeling overpowered by an addiction to pornography or lust and other perversions.

- Inability to get married or marriages ending in divorce.
- No affection or sexual drive for their human spouse.

Open Doors for This Kind of Attack

- **Witchcraft**: Witchcraft potions, love potions or spells that are cast by someone to gain your love or affection leave an open door for a spiritual spouse to attach itself to you.
- **Sexual Sins**: Any form of sexual sin or perversion is one of the most common open doors for a spiritual spouse to lay its hand over you. These sexual sins could be anything from fornication, adultery, bestiality, homosexuality, or any other sexual acts including viewing and consuming pornography. This is almost like their breeding ground, as these demons have an insatiable appetite for sexual perversion and sexual immorality.
- **Generational spirit spouses**: In some cases, *spirit husbands/spirit wives* attach themselves to a bloodline from one generation to another. This essentially occurs in cases where someone in the previous generation was involved in witchcraft, sexual perversion, rape, molestation, or human sacrifice.
- **Molestation or Abuse**: While it doesn't sound fair, demons view the act of molestation or abuse as an

open door and often, already associated with the sexual perversion of the molester, they attach themselves to the victims of sexual abuse.

- **Soul Ties**: When the person that you have a soul tie with walks away from your life, it results in the breaking of your soul into fragments. The enemy takes advantage of this weak point and comes in as a spirit spouse.

Do you acknowledge that you are experiencing symptoms of the spirit of Rejection?

Circle One

Yes, or No?

If yes, what are the symptoms?

....

....

....

....

....

....

....

....

....

Please write out your acceptance declaration in the space provided below.

....
....
....
....
....
....
....
....
....
....

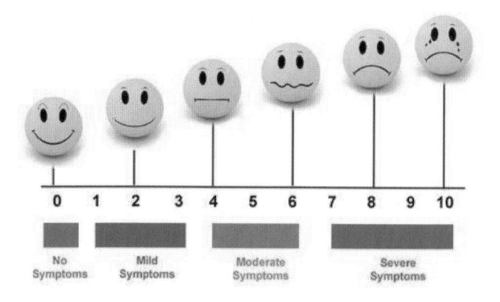

ZERO BEING THE LEAST AND TEN BEING THE MAX, HOW DO YOU EVALUATE YOUR SITUATION?

Please circle one below

Answer:

- A) No Symptoms
- B) Mild Symptoms
- C) Moderate Symptoms
- D) Severe Symptoms

EXECUTION

Time to execute your strategies to break free

....
....
....
....
....
....
....
....
....
....

Break Free from a spiritual spouse

Deliverance is your portion.

Living in freedom and deliverance from a spiritual spouse requires a disciplined devotion to God. These are a few things that can help you be free and remain free:

- Follow the Break Free Prayer guide and...
- Go beyond a sinner's prayer or being a lukewarm Christian and **Devote your life to Jesus.**
- Set your body apart and declare it as that which belongs to the Holy Spirit, bought by the blood of Jesus, and **become His temple.**
- **Abort anything planted by the spirit spouse** in your life. Confess, declare, and uproot any seed/offspring planted in your life as a result of the encounters.

If the torment continues, **seek deliverance**. Deliverance prayers, prayer lines, prayers with pastors in the deliverance ministry, deliverance conferences like *Raised to Deliver*, are all means that will take you into an atmosphere of deliverance and you will be set free in our Lord.

Acknowledgment

The following statement has been proven true- you will never pursue change unless you first acknowledge the need to. The word acknowledge means, to accept or admit the existence or truth of. Truth disregarded will serve as a continuation of bondage. It is therefore important for you to first acknowledge the areas in your life and family where break free is needed. Although it has the potential to be painful, you might want to look closely at the negative patterns of your family as a starting point.

Acceptance

Acceptance is the ability to see things as they are in the present. Sooner than later, we must come to terms with things as they are and accept them, despite how difficult it may be because it is necessary to our Break Free.

Tip

Breaking free from limitations is often seen as a spiritual passage, as it involves a deeper exploration of one's beliefs, thoughts, and emotions.

In this section, I have provided additional worksheets for you to write down other limitations that you believe you are battling against. I also provided additional action plans as your guide.

ACKNOWLEDGEMENT OF LIMITATIONS

ACCEPTANCE OF LIMITATIONS

ACKNOWLEDGMENT OF LIMITATIONS

STEPHANIE MCKIE

ACCEPTANCE OF LIMITATIONS

ACTION PLAN

1. **You are not your limitations:** One of the most important spiritual truths about breaking free from limitations is to recognize that you are not defined by your limitations. Your limitations are simply a product of the spiritual attacks raised against you. However, now that you understand how the realm of the spirit works you now realize that you are not your limitations, you can start to shift your focus towards your potential and limitless possibilities by adapting the Break Free guidelines in this book.

2. **Everything is possible:** Another spiritual truth about breaking free from limitations is that everything is possible. When you believe in yourself and the power of God, you can overcome any obstacle and achieve anything you set your mind to. This requires a shift in perspective from seeing limitations as only natural start but spiritual ones and addressing them as such.

3. **You are connected to someone greater:** When you embark on a journey of breaking free from limitations, you may realize that you are connected to someone greater than yourself- who is God Almighty. When you tap into this connection, you

can draw strength and inspiration to overcome your limitations.

4. Letting go is key: Letting go of limiting beliefs, fears, and attachments is an essential part of breaking free from limitations. When you release what no longer serves you, you make space for new possibilities and experiences to come into your life.

5. You are worthy of living a fulfilling life: It is important to recognize that you are worthy of living a fulfilling life, free from limitations. When you believe in your own worthiness, you can start to take action towards creating the life you desire and breaking free from any limitations that are holding you back.

Let's look at some causes of the spirit of limitation entering our lives.

Past Sins

Breaking free from past sins can be challenging but necessary.

On the worksheet provided on the next page, please record any past sins that you believe you need to Break Free from.

WHAT ARE THE PAST SINS YOU NEED TO BREAK FREE FROM?

....
....
....
....
....
....
....
....
....
....
....
....
....
....
....
....
....
....
....
....
....
....
....
....

WHAT ARE THE PAST SINS YOU NEED TO BREAK FREE FROM?

ACCEPTANCE OF PAST SINS

ACTION PLAN

1. Forgiveness is key: One of the most important spiritual truths about breaking free from past sins is that forgiveness is key. This means forgiving yourself for the mistakes you have made and forgiving others who may have hurt you. When you forgive, you release the negative energy associated with past sins and create space for healing and growth.

2. Repentance is necessary: Repentance is an important part of breaking free from past sins. This means acknowledging the harm you have caused, expressing remorse, and making amends. When you take responsibility for your actions and seek to make things right, you can begin to move forward.

3. You are not defined by your past mistakes: While your past may have shaped you, it does not have to dictate your future. When you recognize that you have the power to change your thoughts, beliefs, and actions, you can create a new reality for yourself.

4. Grace and mercy are available: This means that even if you feel unworthy or undeserving of forgiveness, you can still receive it. When you open yourself up to grace and mercy, you allow yourself to be transformed and renewed.

5. Letting go is necessary: Letting go of past sins is an essential part of breaking free from them. When you hold onto guilt, shame, or regret, you are perpetuating the negative energy associated with past sins. Letting go allows you to move forward with a lighter heart and a clearer mind.

Here is another entry for the spirit of limitation

Fear

Breaking free from fear involves a deeper exploration of one's beliefs, thoughts, and emotions.

On the worksheet provided on the next page, please record any fear that you believe you need to Break Free from.

WHAT ARE YOUR FEARS?

....
....
....
....
....
....
....
....
....
....
....
....
....
....
....
....
....
....
....
....
....
....
....
....

WHAT ARE YOUR FEARS?

STEPHANIE MCKIE

ACCEPTANCE OF FEARS

THE BREAK FREE WORKBOOK

ACTION PLAN

1. Fear can be conquered: Fear is often based on our perceptions and beliefs, and not necessarily on reality. When we recognize that fear is not always based on truth, we can start to challenge our thoughts and beliefs that are causing fear. Follow the Break Free prayer guide to help break fear.

2. Love is the opposite of fear: Another spiritual truth about breaking free from fear is that love is the opposite of fear. When we focus on love, we can start to shift our energy away from fear. This means cultivating love for us, others, and the world around us.

3. Courage comes from within: Courage is an essential part of breaking free from fear. When we recognize that courage comes from within, we can start to tap into our inner strength and power. This means taking action even when we feel afraid and facing our fears head-on.

4. Trust in God: This means recognizing that we are not alone, and that there is a greater power at work on our side. When we trust in God, we can feel a

sense of comfort and security, even in the face of fear.

5. Mindfulness can help: Mindfulness is a powerful tool for breaking free from fear. When we practice mindfulness, we can observe our thoughts and emotions without judgment. This means we can recognize when we are feeling afraid and respond with compassion and curiosity rather than reacting with fear.

Another entry for the spirit of limitation to enter our lives

Sexual Abuse

Breaking free from sexual abuse is a deeply personal and complex journey, and it may involve a range of physical, emotional, and spiritual healing.

On the worksheet provided on the next page, please record any sexual abuse that you believe you need to Break Free from.

WHAT SEXUAL ABUSE YOU ENCOUNTERED?

WHAT SEXUAL ABUSE YOU ENCOUNTERED?

....
....
....
....
....
....
....
....
....
....
....
....
....
....
....
....
....
....
....
....
....
....
....
....
....

ACCEPTANCE OF SEXUAL ABUSE

ACTION PLAN

1. In addition to the Break Free Prayer guide, seek professional help: It is important to seek the help of a qualified mental health professional who specializes in trauma and abuse. A therapist can provide support, guidance, and tools to help you heal from the trauma of sexual abuse.

2. Build a support system: Surround yourself with supportive friends, family members, or community members who can provide emotional support and encouragement. Joining a support group for survivors of sexual abuse can also be helpful.

3. Practice self-care: Connect to activities that foster physical and emotional interests, such as training, beneficial eating, concentration, and passing time in nature. Practicing self-care can help you to control stress and anxiety, and boost healing and recovery.

4. Explore spirituality: Many survivors of sexual abuse find comfort and healing in exploring their spirituality. This involve connecting with God through prayer, worship, the Word and fasting.

5. Speak out: Breaking the silence about sexual abuse can be a powerful step towards healing and empowerment. This may involve speaking with a trusted friend or family member or seeking support from a local advocacy organization.

It is important to remember that healing from sexual abuse is a process that may take time and effort, but with the right support and resources, it is possible to break free from the effects of sexual abuse and live a fulfilling and empowered life.

POVERTY

Breaking free from poverty is a journey, and it may take time and effort to achieve financial stability. However, with persistence and dedication, it is possible to improve your financial situation and create a brighter future for yourself and your loved ones.

On the worksheet provided on the next page, please record any poverty lifestyle that you believe you need to Break Free from.

WHAT HAS POVERTY HINDERED YOU FROM DOING?

WHAT HAS POVERTY HINDERED YOU FROM DOING?

STEPHANIE MCKIE

ACCEPTANCE OF POVERTY

ACTION PLAN

1. In addition to the Break Free Prayer guide, seek the Lord about your financial situation. Wait for His directives and then pursue. Remember, faith without works is dead.

2. Create a budget: Creating a budget is a crucial first step towards breaking free from poverty. A budget will help you to track your expenses and income, identify areas where you can cut back, and set financial goals.

3. Increase your income: Look for ways to increase your income, such as taking on a part-time job, starting a side hustle, or pursuing education or training that can lead to higher-paying work.

4. Reduce expenses: Look for ways to reduce your expenses, such as cutting back on unnecessary purchases, finding ways to save on household expenses, and shopping for deals and discounts.

5. Build up your reserves: Start increasing your reserves by allocating a specific amount of money each month. This can prove beneficial and possibly cushion you in case of urgent situations. This can

also help you to work towards long-term financial goals.

6. Seek assistance: There are many resources available to help those living in poverty, such as government assistance programs, nonprofit organizations, and community resources. Do not be afraid to seek out help when you need it.

7. Cultivate a positive mindset: Finally, it is important to cultivate a positive mindset and a sense of hope for the future. Believe that you can break free from poverty and work towards your goals with determination and perseverance.

FAILURE

Breaking free from failure is a journey that requires self-compassion, self-reflection, and a willingness to learn and grow from setbacks.

On the worksheet provided on the next page, please record any failure you have encountered that you believe you need to Break Free from.

WHAT ARE SOME FAILURES YOU EXPERIENCED?

WHAT ARE SOME FAILURES YOU EXPERIENCED?

ACCEPTANCE OF FAILURES

ACTION PLAN

1. In addition to the Break Free Prayer guide, practice self-compassion: Be kind and understanding towards yourself when you experience failure. Recognize that failure is a natural part of the learning process and use it as an opportunity for growth and improvement.

2. Reframe your mindset: Reframe your mindset towards failure by viewing it as an opportunity for growth and learning, rather than a reflection of your worth or abilities.

3. Learn from your mistakes: Take the time to reflect on what went wrong and what you can learn from your mistakes. Use this knowledge to adjust and try again.

4. Set realistic goals: Set realistic goals that challenge you but are achievable. Split larger goals into smaller, controllable measures and celebrate your success along the way.

5. Embrace uncertainty: Recognize that success is not always a straight path, and that setbacks and obstacles are part of the journey. Embrace uncertainty

and be open to pivoting or adjusting your approach when necessary.

6. Take action: Take action towards your goals and focus on the process rather than the outcome. Celebrate the small wins along the way and use them as motivation to keep going.

Never forget- catastrophe is not the reverse of success, but rather a step towards it. Embrace the lessons that failure can teach you and use them to propel you toward greater success in the future.

FAMILY & RELATIONSHIP HURTS

Breaking free from family hurts can be difficult but it is important to prioritize your own well-being and emotional health.

On the worksheet provided on the next page, please record any family or relationship hurt that you believe you need to Break Free from.

WHAT ARE THE FAMILY AND RELATIONSHIP HURTS YOU HAVE ENCOUNTERED?

WHAT ARE THE FAMILY AND RELATIONSHIP HURTS YOU HAVE ENCOUNTERED?

....
....
....
....
....
....
....
....
....
....
....
....
....
....
....
....
....
....
....
....
....
....

THE BREAK FREE WORKBOOK

ACCEPTANCE OF FAMILY HURTS

ACTION PLAN

1. Follow the Break Free Prayer guide.

2. Be honest with God about the hurts you have suffered.

3. Acknowledge your feelings: Allow yourself to feel your emotions and acknowledge the pain that has been caused. Recognize that your feelings are valid and that it's okay to grieve the loss of the family relationship you may have wanted or expected.

4. Set boundaries: It is important to set boundaries with family members who have hurt you in order to protect yourself emotionally. This may involve limiting contact or taking a break from the relationship altogether.

5. Seek support: Surround yourself with supportive friends or a therapist who can provide a safe space to process your emotions and experiences.

6. Practice forgiveness: Forgiveness is not about excusing hurtful behavior or minimizing your pain, but rather about releasing yourself from the anger and resentment that can hold you back.

Forgiveness can be a difficult and ongoing process, but it can be an important step towards healing.

7. Focus on self-care: Take care of yourself emotionally, physically, and spiritually. Engage in activities that bring you joy and help you to feel grounded and centered, such as meditation, exercise, or spending time in nature.

Remember that healing from family hurt is a journey, and it may take time and effort to process your emotions and move forward. Be patient with yourself and prioritize your own well-being as you work towards healing and finding peace.

DEPRESSION

Breaking free from depression can be difficult. Recovery from depression is a journey, and it may take time and effort to find the right combination of treatments and strategies that work for you. Be patient with yourself, and don't be afraid to seek out the support and resources you need to improve your mental health and well-being.

On the worksheet provided on the next page, please record any depression symptoms that you may be experiencing that you need to Break Free from.

ARE YOU DEPRESSED? IF YES, WHAT ARE THE CAUSES OF YOUR DEPRESSION?

....
....
....
....
....
....
....
....
....
....
....
....
....
....
....
....
....
....
....
....
....
....
....

ARE YOU DEPRESSED? IF YES, WHAT ARE THE CAUSES OF YOUR DEPRESSION?

....
....
....
....
....
....
....
....
....
....
....
....
....
....
....
....
....
....
....
....
....
....
....
....

STEPHANIE MCKIE

ACCEPTANCE OF DEPRESSION

ACTION PLAN

1. God is the master healer and is willing to heal you from depression. Speak to Him and follow the Break Free Prayer guide.

2. Seek professional help: Depression is a serious mental health condition, and it is important to seek professional help from a therapist, psychiatrist, or other mental health professional. They can provide you with the support and resources you need to manage your symptoms and work towards recovery.

3. Practice self-care: Take care of yourself emotionally, physically, and spiritually. This may include getting enough sleep, eating a healthy diet, engaging in regular exercise, and finding ways to manage stress and anxiety.

4. Develop a support network: Reach out to friends and family members who can provide you with emotional support and encouragement. Consider joining a support group for individuals with depression to connect with others who may be experiencing similar struggles.

5. Challenge negative thoughts: Depression can be accompanied by negative self-talk and distorted thinking patterns. Work with a therapist to challenge these negative thoughts and reframe them in a more positive and realistic way.

6. Set achievable goals: Set achievable goals for yourself that are specific, measurable, and realistic. Celebrate your progress along the way and don't be too hard on yourself if you experience setbacks.

7. Consider medication: In some cases, medication may be necessary to manage symptoms of depression. Talk to a mental health professional or your doctor about whether medication may be a helpful treatment option for you.

MISCELLANEOUS

So far, you might not have seen the area you need help with listed. Follow the sequence of acknowledging, acceptance, and action plan. Below are pages provided for you to do your recordings.

ACKNOWLEDGE

ACCEPTANCE

THE BREAK FREE WORKBOOK

ACTION PLAN

ACKNOWLEDGE

ACCEPTANCE

THE BREAK FREE WORKBOOK

ACTION PLAN

ACKNOWLEDGE

ACCEPTANCE

THE BREAK FREE WORKBOOK

ACTION PLAN

MAINTENANCE

The account of St. John according to the eighth chapter, speaks sternly about maintenance.

> *"And the scribes and Pharisees brought unto him a woman taken in adultery; and when they had set her in the midst,*
> *They say unto him, Master, this woman was taken in adultery, in the very act. Now Moses in the law commanded us, that such should be stoned: but what sayest thou? This they said, tempting him, that they might have to accuse him. But Jesus stooped down, and with **his** finger wrote on the ground, **as though he heard them not**. So when they continued asking him, he lifted up himself, and said unto them, He that is without sin among you, let him first cast a stone at her. And again he stooped down, and wrote on the ground. And they which heard **it**, being convicted by **their own** conscience, went out one by one, beginning at the eldest, **even unto** the last: and Jesus was left alone, and the woman standing in the midst. When Jesus had lifted up himself, and saw none but the woman, he said unto her, Woman, where are those thine accusers? hath no man condemned thee? She said, No man, Lord. And Jesus said unto her, neither do I condemn thee: go, and sin no more."*

Essentially Jesus said to her, go and maintain your deliverance. You should be dead, but grace and mercy has given you another opportunity to live. However, this requires maintenance. Maintenance discusses the manner of keeping something in suitable condition or functional order. It encompasses taking steps to prevent or address problems, such as drifting, returning to past weaknesses and prisons. This means cleaning and regular upkeep. By performing regular maintenance, you can help ensure that things continue to work properly and last longer.

Having gone through your break-free, maintenance is vitally important.

To stay spiritually free, you must work at it regularly. Here are some things you can do:

1. Be consistent in prayer and pray the word of God always: Do things that help you feel more connected to God like deep meditation on the way of the Lord. Pray, fast, worship, and study the word of God.

2. Be frequent to the house of God. Get involved in the ministries of your local church.

3. Get to know yourself: Think about your thoughts, feelings, and actions, and be honest with yourself about what you need to improve.

4. Pay attention: Be present and focused on the present moment.

5. Spend time with positive people: Surround yourself with people who make you feel good about yourself and

help to keep you grounded in the Word. Avoid negative people who bring you down.

6. Be intentional: Make clear goals for yourself and make choices that will help you achieve those goals.

7. Be thankful: Think about the good things in your life and be thankful for them.

Remember that staying spiritually free takes effort, but it is worth it. With practice, you can live a happier and more fulfilling life. Always remember the spirit realm supersedes the physical realm.

OTHER STEPS TO MAINTAIN YOUR BREAK FREE

THE BREAK FREE WORKBOOK

𝔇eclarations:

1. I decree and declare that I am determined to Break Free in the Mighty Name of Jesus Christ of Nazareth!

2. I decree and declare that I will always remember, that the fight is never against my brothers and sisters, but according to Ephesians 6: 12, the war is against principalities, against powers, against the rulers of the darkness of this world, against spiritual wickedness in high places; therefore, I will now channel the fight against the devil and his agents, and no more against my brothers and sisters.

3. I decree and declare that I will no longer be ignorant of the stratagems of the devil and his evil powers, but I will always be vigilant to his devices, so I may not be overtaken by his powers anymore (2 Corinthians 2:11).

4. I decree and declare that I will always be reminded that Luke 10: 19 tells me, that God has given unto me the power to tread on serpents and scorpions, and over all the power of the enemy: and nothing shall by any means hurt me. Therefore, I do believe this because God said it, and His word cannot lie,

and because of that, I am beginning to live my life accordingly.

5. I decree and declare that the spirit of complacency, unforgiveness and jealousy, etc. will be no more or will never have a place in my life from this day onwards.

6. I decree and declare that I am intentional that I am strong in the power and might of the Lord and I am putting on the whole armor of God which is His Word so I may not again be entangled in the yoke of bondage.

7. I decree and declare that I am determined about maintaining my deliverance that I have received through the teachings of God's holy words and through His power and might.

8. I decree and declare that I am now the destiny changer in my bloodline, the lives of my children, my marriage, my businesses, my job, and all other aspects in my life.

9. I decree and declare that I am determined to be loving, caring and kind to my brothers and sisters. I will not envy anyone, but I will trust in the Lord my God and wait on his fulfilment in my life, while I work consistently and assiduously to become a better person for my family, my children, my ministry, my society, and myself.

10. I decree and declare that my days of captivity are finally over, and my freedom is now in Jesus Christ mighty name!

BREAK FREE

CONCLUSION

The presence of bondage or imprisonment gives rise to the need to break free. The failure to pursue break free by those who have been illegally restrained, whether spiritually or physically, will result in the continuation of the person's state as is. Therefore, one should always consistently analyze where he or she is spiritually and if acknowledges that there are limitations present, he or she must be intentional and take the necessary steps to Break Free.

ABOUT THE AUTHOR

Stephanie Mckie is a passionate and anointed woman of God whom God has raised up in His Kingdom for such a time as this. She carries both the pastoral and prophetic Grace. She is the co-founder of Kingdom Power and Faith Global; Healing, Restoration and Prophetic Ministries, located in West Palm Beach Florida, USA. She is a past student at Glad Tidings Institute and graduated with her Bachelor's degree in Christian Education and her Doctorate in Theology and Humanities.

Stephanie Mckie is also the founder of "Break Free", an international conference and outreach ministry which is designed to break spiritual strongholds and set the captives free through the power of the Holy Spirit. She has an unwavering faith in God and believes that with God all things are possible. Her favorite quote is, "Everything first happens in the spiritual realm before manifesting on earth. Therefore, always seek to understand about the spiritual realm so we can take authority over our lives."

THE BREAK FREE WORKBOOK

BREAKFREE PRAYER:

Please scan QR Code to Listen to Break Fee Prayer from Dr. Stephanie Mckie.

REFERENCES:

https://blog.biblesforamerica.org

https://www.biblegateway.com/

https://agodman.com

https://citychurchkla.wordpress.com

https://newcreeations.org/difference-between-soul-and-spirit/

https://www.curtlandry.com/battle-the-spirit-of-rejection/

https://pastorvlad.org/spiritualspouses/

https://www.activechristians.org.uk/prayer-watches1/third-watch-12am-to-3am

https://assets.speakcdn.com/assets/1927/prayer_fasting5.pdf

Images:

www.google.com

Made in the USA
Columbia, SC
31 October 2023